The Middlescence Manifesto©

Barbara Waxman MS, MPA, PCC

The Middlescence Factor
P.O. Box 133
Kentfield, CA 94914
www.barbarawaxman.com

Publisher's Note: Names, places, and incidents have been changed to protect the privacy of individuals. Stories have been used with their permission.

Book Layout © 2014 BookDesignTemplates.com

The Middlescence Manifesto/Barbara Waxman -- 1st ed.
ISBN-13: 978-0-9982274-0-5
ISBN-10: 0-9982274-0-4

Tell me,
what is it you plan to do
with your one wild and precious life?

MARY OLIVER

The Middlescence Manifesto

Table of Contents

Chapter 1

A Prescription for Change

I've spent most of my career listening to people at the midpoint of their lives, helping them make sense of where they are and where they're going. I've had the privilege of working with people struggling to make ends meet and others finding themselves struggling with how to lead their lives when earning money is no longer the goal; I've worked with people transitioning careers and others launching and leading multi-national companies; I've worked with the famous and not so famous. What I know to be true is that we are not so very different. As a coach, I've guided them towards an understanding of how they arrived at this point, and helped them tap into their best selves, their vitality, and their potential to become the people they believe they are meant to be. In doing so, I began to notice patterns. Many of my clients used the same language and expressed the same feelings. Even those of extraordinarily high achievement reported feeling lost, as though something was missing from their lives. Stunningly pervasive was the reality that people don't understand **that we continue to develop as adults**—or even that adult development exists.

As a trained gerontologist, I was struck by how this rich client data dovetailed with a demographic shift in the United States. Since 1900, we've increased our life expectancy from 47 years to nearly 80. People who are college-educated, non-smokers, and exercise regularly can expect to live even longer. Yet somehow we're still stuck, thinking that 65 is old and that the years that precede it are the slippery slope to decline. Many of us have heard statistics that we're living longer, but have assumed that we've added those additional years at the end of life, when we're "old."

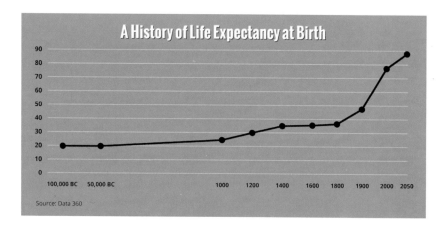

That's simply not true. Thanks to advances in sanitation, medicine, and nutrition, we've added meaningful decades to the *middle* of life, not the end. **We've added more years of living, not dying**. And the living we're doing is distinct from that of our parents and grandparents. According to the U.S. Census Bureau, the number of Americans living into their nineties is expected to quadruple by 2050. So if you're 45, you may have half your life ahead of you. Why on earth would you stop creating and discovering, when you're just getting started?

The problem lies, in large part, in our perception of life stages. As a culture, our thinking is stuck in the last century, when we followed a fairly consistent—and predictable—life script: Go to school. Find a job. Get married. Have children. Work hard. Retire. And finally, if you're lucky, maybe find some leisure activities and bide your time until death comes calling. That model has gone the way of the rotary phone, but the corresponding mindset hasn't gone with it. The result is a cultural lag, a needless dissonance between perception and reality.

This disconnect is rooted in the language we choose and the attitudes we espouse about what it means to be a full-fledged adult. For years I've listened to my clients echo back the myths perpetuated in popular culture. They ask me, "Isn't my story already written?" "I've invested in many significant life choices I made years ago; is it too late to change?" "Dare I rock the boat?" Or else they worry about the people depending on them to stay the same: "Won't I be letting them down?" My clients tell me, "I feel like I'm at a crossroads; in some ways like I did when I was starting out. Isn't it a little late for me to be feeling this way? How do I let go of old habits and silence my inner critic?"

"Current life structures, career paths, educational choices and social norms are out of alignment with the emerging reality of longer life spans."

Lynda Gratton, Fellow, World Economic Forum

Consider current trends: Roughly one-third of the United States—more than 100 million people—is over the age of 50. Yet ageism runs rampant, a strangely acceptable set of demographic stereotypes perpetuating prejudice against full-fledged adults, and reflecting our culture's obsession with youth. Young people are apt to describe anyone over 40 as "slow" because they don't adopt changing technology as quickly as digital natives. Comedians feel comfortable making sport of "senior moments" and using older people as the butt of their jokes —it's important to be able to take a joke, but it's also important to recognize when a joke is no longer funny.

Ageism isn't just oppressive; it's bad for business, as well as society at large. Overemphasizing youth in the workplace limits diversity, which creates a brain drain and impedes a business' creative output and the breadth of its aptitude for problem solving. To organizations like the Peace Corps, this is old news. Despite the perception that Peace Corps volunteer work is for young adults, the lauded not-for-profit goes out of its way to attract volunteers who are what I refer to as midlife and better.

"In the Peace Corps, [older volunteers'] lifelong learning and professional experience will be an asset in your host country."

Peace Corps site

The arrow of ageism is something we also aim at ourselves. It's a form of self-sabotage. When we buy into these stereotypes, we limit our choices, generate obstacles, and even inhibit our personal growth and happiness. We hit our 40s, and either we don't know what to think, or we feel that we're beginning to shift to the dark side. It's demoralizing and inaccurate.

From a sociological perspective, we're experiencing what's called a *cultural lag*. Our stereotype-driven expectations regarding aging are based on old news, on demographic data from a different era.

> *"There's no desire to be an adult. Adulthood is not a goal. It's not seen as a gift. Something happened culturally: No one is supposed to age past 45—sartorially, cosmetically, attitudinally. Everybody dresses like a teenager. Everybody dyes their hair. Everybody is concerned about a smooth face."*
>
> *Frances McDormand, 2014 profile in the New York Times*

What if we bring our mentality up to date? What if we change our perception of what it *means* to be an adult in midlife? It's time to re-think—or, as my son Matt more accurately says: "It's time to re-brand midlife." I have; it's called **Middlescence.** It's a new life stage for those in midlife, one that takes into account demographic realities of an evolving world, and rejects toxic norms of the past.

Why is this important? Because when you let ageism limit your choices, you limit your potential. The reality for most of us at midlife is that we *need* to work, and *want* to contribute. We have family commitments and financial responsibilities, especially now that we're living longer. Perhaps more importantly we want to continue to lead. When you think about it, we make up the majority of the leaders of our families, communities, businesses and the world. It's not acceptable to let ageist attitudes impede our ability to earn a living, and certainly not to let them detract from the fullness and contentment of our lives. Ageism devalues one of our most important resources— people with experience, knowledge, vitality and the courage to create change.

It's time to shift the paradigm.

My mission is to catalyze a national conversation; to offer the tools for middlescents to thrive, to benefit themselves, their families, communities, and the world.

Chapter 2

Midlife – Perception vs. Reality

Google "Midlife" & Check Out the Images. Go ahead. Do it.

Perception

According to our culture, anyone over the age of about 45 is on the slippery slope towards assisted living. Birthday cards tele-graph that the best years are behind you. Anti-aging products target you.   Articles tell you how to dress appropriately... *for your age.*

It's as though a time bomb went off; suddenly your only choices are retreat, or submission.

Stop fooling yourself.

Reality

It's true that people between about 45-65 years are experiencing *something*. But it's not a crisis, stagnation or decrepitude. Many describe it more as a sense of free-floating anxiety. It's a low-level discontent that keeps us from feeling like we're at the top of our game. And if anything happens to disrupt the order of our lives, we've been taught to believe it's too late to move onto something new, something better.

Clients often tell me that this leads to unexpected feelings of guilt: "I know people who are so much worse off; is it even fair to want more than I already have?" We aren't miserable so asking for help to figure out how to feel authentic, happy, connected and centered often feels like asking for too much. Michael felt this way: he sold the business he had built over the course of 30 years of blood, sweat and tears. He was still happily married to his college sweetheart and had launched two children into the world. He no longer had to work in order to prove anything or to pay the bills—he had plenty. On the outside. But inside he craved something more. He felt out of touch with himself without the context of needing to meet financial goals and raising children. That sensibility and questioning is common even amongst midlife adults who seem to have it all. We second-guess our natural, healthy ambition. We silence or ignore the voice in our heads telling us life keeps changing and we keep growing and learning about ourselves, the world around us and what we really care about today--in this moment.

Research has shown that even controlling for financial resources, employment status and children, our levels of self-reported happiness dip to the lowest point in our mid-40's. There is a mental picture we often have when we are young about how our life will turn out. It looks like a straight-line graph that gets better and better—but that's never the case.

"We are all born with a great dream for our lives," explained cultural anthropologist Angeles Arrien in the forward of her book, *The Second Half of Life: Opening the Eight Gates of Wisdom,* "a dream that may have been derailed along the way by family and career responsibilities or submerged by our own choices."

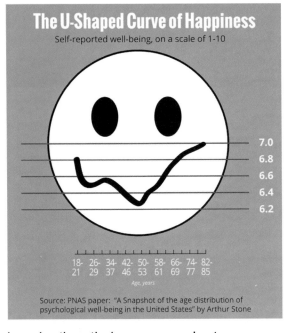

Source: PNAS paper: "A Snapshot of the age distribution of psychological well-being in the United States" by Arthur Stone

Research suggests that realization of that original dream has little to do with our happiness later in life. We find new dreams, and new, unexpected sources of joy. Far from being unhappy, a Harris Poll found that adults over 50 are more likely to be happier than their younger cohort.

Given our cultural perception of aging, some people might be surprised that *happiness increases after age 50,* particularly when it dips so low in our 40's. My training and experience have taught me that this phenomenon is closely related to our ability to reconcile the give and take of this stage of life.

Our Bodies

Yes, it's a bummer: We lose muscle mass at a rate of 3-5 percent every decade after turning 40. We get injured more easily. We have more trouble losing weight. And we have to be careful about our cholesterol and blood sugar. Gone are the days when we could go for a ten-mile early morning run and follow it with a breakfast of donuts. On the bright side, many of the injuries that may have devastated us in the past are, today, merely passing hiccups in the ongoing narrative of our physical lives. At 53 I was living the dream, living and working in Italy with my husband. Towards the end of our year there I began experiencing tremendous pain in my hip; not wanting to detract from the year we'd planned for a decade I trudged on. Upon our return I quickly learned I needed to have a complete hip replacement. So I get it--physical changes associated with aging are hard. But we now have the technology and information to take the challenges of wear and tear and help ourselves remain incredibly active, energetic and vital.

Another effect of our changing bodies is that we may struggle with self-image—haven't we always? The difference now is that as we get older, our physical beauty changes in ways that society hasn't embraced. How about *trading in* some of our old notions of beauty? When we do so, we can *trade up* from insecurity about our appearance to a refreshing sense of self-acceptance and self-confidence.

This was driven home to me last summer in Italy. We visited a crowded beach that's generally only frequented by locals. Shockingly (to me, anyway), only two women on the beach were wearing one-piece bathing suits: An octogenarian and myself! I asked a number of Italians about this and they told me that not only did they accept that all bodies are different, but that they also differed by age. They found our American idea of "deserving to wear a two-piece bathing suit" ridiculous.

Later that day, I bought a bikini.

Loss

Changes to our bodies are not the only struggles we face in middlescence. With every passing year we are further confronted by our own mortality, and that of those we love. As the invincibility of our youth fades, we're more likely to experience loss. We may battle illness or be involved in serious accidents. And even if we personally are lucky enough to avoid such things, we're almost certain to see them afflicting our parents, friends, and family members.

There is sadness in this loss. But there is also something we have that youth just doesn't provide: a precious, deeply held recognition that every day is a gift. From this perspective, we're better able to savor life's moments and the people who make them special. Perhaps that recognition helps explain the evidence that middlescence can be amongst the happiest, most content years of our lives.

It largely depends on where you choose to place your focus. Losses happen. But at this stage, you're more likely to have the resources and judgment to navigate life's ups and downs. You know what is valuable to you—family, friends, health, giving— and what's not. You've accumulated decades of expertise and experience, and you're ready to manage and lead people and organizations. Sometimes, the most horrific losses can fuel a hunger for honoring our loved one's by living fully.

> *"I do think that loss is something that comes with this period of life. You start seeing it. Parents, health issues, whatever. It's a lot harder to take things for granted like you did when you were 25 or 30. I'd love to spend more quality time with friends . . . I've always worked, and at this stage of my life--in my 50s-- I will definitely sacrifice a paying client for a friend, and make that time, because I see how valuable that time is.*
>
> *Lisa, an accountant in her early 50s who went back to school and studied coaching and nutrition.*

All of this brings us back to the U-shaped graph that shows us a steady rise in self-reported contentment after age 50. If this is our reality—that midlife actually begins a new stage of increased happiness and personal satisfaction—why aren't we all experiencing it and reveling in it? Why don't we look forward to and celebrate this time of life?

Perhaps because we haven't been given reason for optimism. We're led to believe that by the time we reach midlife, it's nearly impossible to reevaluate our stories and write new, divergent chapters for the future. And if we *do* decide to make a change, it needs to be either a "sure thing," or else in pursuit of a lofty, often unattainable goal. Society tells us it's too late to take risks—to try something new without a guarantee of success—just because we want to. If we do we're often labeled as having a midlife crisis.

Over and over again, working with clients and sharing stories with friends and family, I've found that society's got it all wrong.

Terry's story is reminiscent of so many clients: A few years ago, in his late 50's, he made a decision that would baffle anyone living with the antiquated mindset that our 40's or 50's mark the beginning of the end. Terry was a financial services executive, and found that his job was giving him too much stress and too little in the way of meaning, purpose, and financial stability. He wanted to believe there was something more. So, after a great deal of deliberation, Terry channeled the courage that lies within all of us, and made the decision to start a new career in the aviation industry, which had always fascinated him. In fact, he earned his pilot's license and lived for the freedom he felt in the sky. But he had virtually no experience working in that field. He worked hard, paid his dues and eventually took over a Cessna dealership. And on top of that, he did it during what he now describes as "one of the most challenging times in US history [to sell] discretionary vehicles."

I love Terry's story because it's real; nothing came easily for him—not the decision to change careers, nor the change itself. But he did it. I caught up with Terry recently and he filled me in on new developments:

"My wife and I moved to Houston in April to represent a manufacturer here. After six really hard years, I feel like I have passed the test and I'm enjoying a great opportunity. ...I'm super optimistic... the struggles are going to pay off with a successful relationship with a new and highly respected aircraft manufacturer."

Terry's story reinforces what I hope will one day become an obvious, unimpeachable reality—that the middle years of our lives are perfectly suited for change and experimentation. The opportunities of contemporary midlife are unprecedented.

Chapter 3

Redefining Life Stages

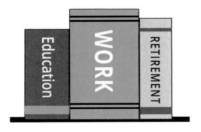

We're on a road, but our map is outdated. We don't know what to expect because we don't know what's possible—or worse, we *think* we know what to expect, but our notions are defined by antiquated stereotypes of the past. No generation has experienced the benefits of increased life expectancy and the potential for undiminished vitality in the way that we can. By redefining the midlife stage, we redefine *all* the life stages that surround it. Old constructs no longer apply. We are trailblazers.

(Formerly Known as) Retirement
In 2006 I was Special Editor of the popular book, *How to Love Your Retirement.* Though the book has since been reprinted and expanded, the first sentence of the first edition is as true

now as when I wrote it: "Here's a little secret: There is no such thing as retirement anymore!"

The goal line of retirement hasn't just moved; it's disappeared. It's true that many of us can't afford to retire; it's also true that most of us have no interest in completely leaving meaningful paid and volunteer work—we just don't want to feel beholden to it like we did for years.

A recent study by the Center for Retirement Research at Boston College noted, "Working provides people with substantial financial, psychosocial and cognitive resources to draw upon, while retirement can create stress, anxiety and even depression, especially in countries where work is highly valued."

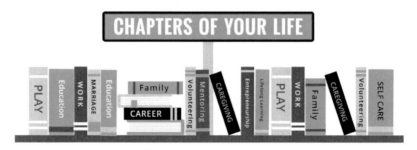

Consider the statement above, and then consider that in the past century alone, we have added about three decades to our life expectancy. And make no mistake; that time is not merely tacked on to the end of our lives, 30 extra years of infirmity. It is an opportunity for us to follow Terry's path and explore new options inherent in these reshaped and expanded life stages.

(Formerly known as) Midlife

This fundamental alteration to the nature of retirement reverberates throughout the years that precede it. Midlife, once a promise and possibility.

No previous generation has experienced the luxury of extended vitality through midlife.

There's a reason for this. For hundreds of thousands of years people didn't age – they died as the result of accidents, disease and more. As recently as the 20th century, the "middle years" were around age 24. Compare that to the life expectancy of US babies born today; according to an article appearing in the medical journal The Lancet, more than half of all babies born in industrialized nations since 2000 can expect to live into the triple digits. Midlife doesn't begin until we're in our 40's, and with advances in medicine and our ever-increasing knowledge of healthy lifestyle habits, the life stage carries on well into our 60s.

Chapter 4

What's Next

Far from tacking on decades of senility and decrepitude at the end of life, we've added great periods of time characterized by growth, change and vitality—very different from the way our parents spent their midlife.

These newly found years create opportunities, allowing many of us to pursue different paths. In 2016 a study by *The Allianz Longevity Project*, found that 49% of Americans would prefer to spend their middle years on a non-traditional path that is unique to their interests. **There is a wanderlust happening; people want to create their own roadmaps to a life well-lived.**

The possibilities are exciting. According to a *Harvard Business Review* article by Lynda Gratton and Andrew Scott, professors at the London School of Business, there will be ". . . **an inevitable redesign of work and life.** When people live longer, the arc of their life stretches...the traditional three-stage life will morph into multiple stages containing two, three or even more different careers. Each of these stages could be different. In one, the focus could be on building financial success and personal achievement, in another on creating a better work/life balance, another still on exploring and understanding options more fully... another on making a social contribution."

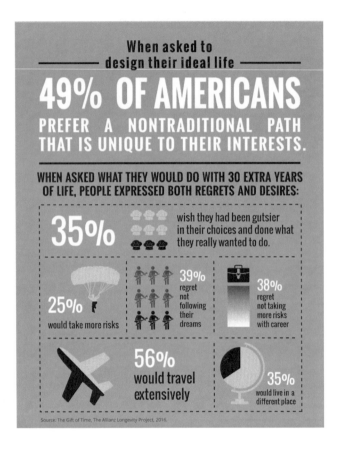

In other words, **our lives are no longer defined by chronological age, but rather by stage, and by the way we feel and the choices ahead of us.**

Peter is another longtime client and financial services executive who opted to make a significant change in his 50s: he went back to school. After earning his master's degree in social work, Peter transitioned to an entirely new industry. In his 60s, he became CEO of a non-profit. "The process," he told me, "was really fun. ...I didn't have a plan, obviously, for the last 20 years to have one career and start a second career. It was more in the moment. ...that's what's really shifted, I think—that people are going to live longer. I just knew I wanted to keep learning and keep contributing, because I had a lot that I thought I could add to my work. It was very intentional. The switch from the private sector was great I would do it again."

We've Created New Life Stages Before

Adolescence was once a *new* life stage too. Identified and named in 1904 by G. Stanley Hall, a pioneer in the study of children, the term *adolescence* arose from shifts in our culture. Before the turn of the century, children were often sent out to work, leaping straight from childhood into adult roles. But policies changed and protections were put in place, creating a period (which included mandatory education) during which this age group could *transition* into adulthood. Recognizing and naming the life stage of adolescence has had a massive impact on our culture, changing the way we experience not only the teenage years that fall under adolescence's umbrella, but all the years that follow.

It's time we do the same for the more than 80 million Americans between the ages of about 45-65.

Like Adolescence – With Wisdom!

Think of middlescence as something akin to a second adolescence.

- Just like adolescence, **our bodies are morphing.** But now, because of shifts in our hormones and wear and tear on our bodies, we require *more* time spent on health and wellness than when we were younger.
- Just like adolescence, **our relationships may be shifting.** We may be empty-nesters, divorcees, caregivers, or even newlyweds. We're finding it's time to revisit and reprioritize our most important relationships, as we're reassessing what's most important to us and who needs us most.
- Just like adolescence, **we have questions about our place in the world** and wonder what our future holds. The life scripts we've been following may no longer feel right. We're learning that decisions made in our 20's don't feel relevant now or for our future. We're no longer young, but we certainly aren't old.
- Just like adolescence, **our sense of self, our identity is evolving.** We crave an understanding of who we want to be when we grow up—even though we're grownups!

This is a new life stage born of our increased longevity. We now live long enough to go through the kinds of life-defining changes associated with adolescence - twice!

What's in a name?

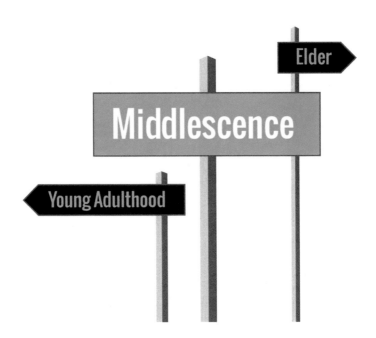

For the second time in recent history, we're experiencing a new stage of life. So why do we still experience it as disorienting and without clear expectations?

The answer is simple: this new life stage has not been named. By naming something, just as we did with adolescence, we bestow upon it power, presence and definition. Naming allows us to understand an idea and create context. Naming midlife—the *new* midlife—will help eradicate the free-floating anxiety many of us feel, creating fertile ground for challenges yes, and also happiness, growth and development.

"I believe in the power and mystery of naming things. Language has the capacity to transform our cells, rear- range our learning, patterns of behavior, and redirect our thinking. I believe in naming what's right in front of us be- cause that is often what is most visible."

Eve Ensler, "This I Believe: The Personal Philosophies of Remarkable Men and Women", playwright, author of the Vagina Monologues

Just as it did for adolescence, naming this new life stage will help to shape the way we approach and experience midlife.

I call it *Middlescence.*

Chapter 5

Middlescence

Middlescence [noun]

pronounced "middle-essence"

A transitional period, between the ages of about 45 and 65, marked by an increased desire to find or create greater meaning in one's life. Often accompanied by physical, social, and economic changes, it is a turning point from which adults continue to develop and grow. A life stage created by increased longevity patterns in the 21st century.

Middlescence: Land of Endless Possibility

By naming middlescence and embracing the philosophy that it is a time of change and potential, we'll create a culture with fewer preconceived notions about aging. We'll live according to what we envision and experience, not according to what's considered acceptable for someone at 45, 55 or 65.

Our joints may be creakier; we may not bounce back after a late night concert like we did in our 20s, but we have create change in and around us.

We cycle in and out of experiences. Some may be stereotypical of midlife. Others may feel more like our youth. What's exciting is that it doesn't matter—no longer must we define our experience by preconceptions of what's appropriate according to the number of a driver's license.

Already, attitudes are beginning to shift. Nearly half of the 3000 respondents in a study conducted by *Allianz* felt that a longer life expectancy would allow them to take a different view of how—and when—major life choices are made. The choice of what we do, and when we do it, is ours.

And choices are good.

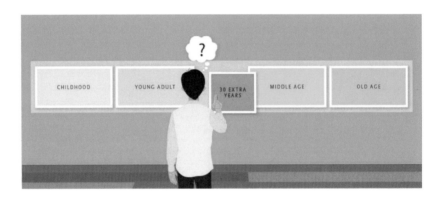

Illustration: Allianz Longevity Project

Of those same Allianz respondents, 32% said that they regretted choices they had made, such as where they attended school, what profession they chose, and where they worked. Middlescence is a chance to change our narrative; we can edit the mistakes of our youth and compose new chapters of healthy risk-taking, unencumbered by (but conscious of) the commitments and responsibilities of our lives.

> *"I wish I could say that I had a vision from college days to where I ended up, but I don't think life really works that way for most of us. Some people grow up, want to be a doctor, become a doctor and build a career. But it was never as clear as that to me. I'd always had a feeling I'd like to run my own business"*
>
> *David, marketing executive who embarked upon entrepreneurship as a middlescent*

Though, for convenience's sake, we often use the age range of 45-65 to describe middlescence, the truth is that defining it with numbers fundamentally contradicts the idea of living our lives in stages. Take the following quiz to see if you fit the bill of a middlescent.

Are You a Middlescent?

Check the descriptions that apply to you and let's see.

_____ I am roughly 45-65 years old.

_____ I feel like I'm ready for some changes in my life but I'm not sure where or how.

_____ Some of the relationships that have been important to me seem to be shifting.

_____ My body is changing—sometimes seemingly overnight—in ways that are a little unsettling.

_____ Sometimes I feel like a teenager with all these hormone changes.

_____ I definitely don't feel old, but I'm certainly not young either.

_____ I'm too *busy* spending time on things that are just not that important to me; I don't think I can keep doing that.

*If at least four of these statements apply to you,
you are experiencing Middlescence.*

The Middlescence Factor[©]

I wrote The Middlescence Manifesto to publicly declare that our culture is lagging and to name life's newest stage. Manifestos are meant to disrupt the current state and create change. I created the Middlescence Factor© to share ideas and provide the tools to help make this happen on an individual and communal level.

The Oxford English Dictionary defines a **factor** as "…a circumstance, fact or influence which contributes to a result or outcome". If accepting middlescence as a life stage and embracing its exciting possibilities is our desired outcome, then **The Middlescence Factor**© is the influence which contributes to [that] result. The Middlescence Factor© is the secret sauce that brings it all together, that uplifts and shifts our consciousness so we can harness the potential of this new stage.

I know that concept may sound a little abstract, so maybe it's easiest to describe with the story of Laura, my very first coaching client, and someone who's passion, real life challenges, and courage embody the Middlescence Factor©.

I met Laura many years ago; our children were in school together. Like many of my clients, Laura wasn't hopeless or lost; in fact, life was pretty good. In 2003, she had just completed a year of training to climb Mt. Shasta. She'd worked for a long time as the head of a fundraising firm, but wanted to spend more time at home with her children. She left that firm and developed her own business. She created a highly successful fundraising firm and struggled with balancing the growth of her company with being the mother she wanted to be. Like a lot of my clients we talked about and experimented with leadership principles and life balance. In the early years we worked together on a weekly basis, defining and activating Laura's plan for her life well-lived.

Tragically, in 2009, Laura's daughter, Lili, passed away at 15 years old. Due in some part to a medical condition, Lili had long experienced social isolation. Now Laura, who had already reimagined her career in middlescence, was sadly primed for another, more dramatic and comprehensive life overhaul. So many of us would have withered after losing a child. Not Laura. With her husband, digging deeper than she ever thought possible, Laura founded the nonprofit *Beyond Differences,* an organization dedicated to ending social isolation among middle school students. After five years, this extraordinary organization had grown to such an extent that serving as its Executive Director became Laura's fulltime job, which it remains today.

I mentioned earlier that I created the Middlescence Factor© to help provide people the ideas and tools to fulfill the promise of middlescence: a life stage of vitality, change, and potential. In the coming pages I'll share one tool and one new approach to living well in middlescence.

First is The Thriving Quiz©. Before we get into the details of the quiz, let's briefly revisit Laura's story. Despite so many challenges, Laura was able to adapt consistently and successfully in middlescence. Much of this, of course, I attribute to her incredible and intangible strength of character and resilience. Not to mention that she had so many meaningful life experiences to draw from: she'd achieved great success working as a fundraiser, then building her own business; and of course her experiences as a mother, wife, and community leader contributed all the more to her strength of character. During my time working with Laura one our primary areas of focus was how to cultivate the lessons of her life experience, along with her energy and vitality, in order to accomplish her goals. This is where the five tenets espoused in the The Thriving Quiz© come into play.

The Thriving Quiz© is the most foundational tool to the Middlescence Factor©. The quiz is based on quantitative research and qualitative experience, and is comprised of scoring yourself on the Five Essentials—
- Physical wellbeing
- Rest and Renewal
- Attention and Focus
- Meaning and Purpose
- Time and Energy Management

For Laura and countless other middlescents who have so much on their plates, it's easy to fall into the trap of believing the most important step towards accomplishing your goals is to manage your time. While time management is of course important, in my experience it's not nearly so valuable as **learning to manage your *energy in the time that you have.***

The Thriving Quiz© provides a comprehensive assessment of the pivotal areas in our lives that help us manage our energy; it tells us where we are succeeding, where there is room for growth, and it provides us a broader view of our energy management as a whole. Take the quiz and determine the specific steps you need to take in order to thrive.

Find the Thriving Quiz at https://barbarawaxman.com/quiz/

Barbara Waxman

Chapter 6

Don't Get Stuck on Purpose

As we maneuver through midlife, we often find ourselves longing for a greater sense of *purpose.* I'd like to share a different approach.

As a culture, we seem to be obsessed with purpose. That's both good and bad. Yes, it's important to have a life rich with meaning. But the pressure we often put on ourselves to find our one calling often leaves us feeling adrift. Popular statements such as "The purpose of life is a life of purpose" often do little more than stress us out.

Having said that, purpose *does* add to the richness of life in middlescence. It can provide greater job satisfaction and increase our performance at work. According to a 2015 survey conducted by Imperative and New York University, *The Workforce Purpose Index*, purpose-driven workers were more likely to be in leadership positions, promote their employees and report higher levels of fulfillment in their jobs.

The same survey found that, beginning at the age of 45, more people begin to report that they feel purpose-focused at work. The problem is that we often blind ourselves to the possibilities right in front of us as we search for the elusive, capital "P" purpose.

Gunther's story provides a great example. Throughout his 20s and 30s, Gunther's life was running smoothly: He was happily married, had two children, lived in a home he loved, and ran marathons. But when he was 43, things started to change. The company he worked for took a nosedive. Without the income he was used to, his confidence was shaken. Finances became a real challenge. He started to feel depressed. As Gunther moved more fully into midlife, he struggled to stay positive as he realized the life he'd planned wasn't the life he was living. A year ago, he sent me this note:

> *You know Barb, when I was younger and newly married, my hopes and dreams were endless... … [now] I find myself thinking my choices are limited; my story is written…*

A month later, we caught up by phone. He called for my advice; his wife had found a two-day retreat on "Finding Your Purpose." It cost $1,000. Money was extremely tight, but she lovingly encouraged him to attend.

He was conflicted. He told me, "I've been so stuck for the past few years. I don't know what I want to do, I can't seem to get going. I need to get back to work with an income but I have a sense that I need to be doing something I care about…at least a little. Maybe I'd find my sense of purpose and get unstuck?"

I said, "Gunther, don't get stuck on Purpose."

I believe that purpose is such a big and lofty concept that it often obstructs what's right in front of us. When we focus solely on finding purpose, we can limit our vision and ability to move forward. The truth is that more often than not, our purpose finds us. It evolves when we live in sync with our values and grow to know ourselves more fully. We can also have more than one purpose. And purpose can change over time.

So I said to Gunther, "Let's talk for a few minutes and see what comes up. Then you can decide about the seminar." We spoke for more than a few minutes.

I will share with you what Gunther and so many other people experience when they let the idea of purpose go. **We uncovered parts of his life he considered interesting but unimportant**—like his love of cigars, golf and designer glasses, for example.

After we spoke, Gunther decided not to attend the seminar but to start experimenting instead. He hadn't worked for quite some time, but now has two gigs—one as an entrepreneur in the cigar industry, and another job in a pro shop, a more stable position where he's learning the ropes, getting a paycheck and playing free rounds of golf in his spare time.

Most importantly he doesn't feel stuck. He's working. And he's happier than he's felt in a long time.

Gunther's story is just one example of how purpose with a *small "p"* can change our lives. When we're motivated by something greater than a paycheck, our lives become more meaningful, we're happier and we're more likely to behave in ways that benefit ourselves, our families, and the world around us.

Purpose Orientation by Age

29%	39%	47%
45-54	55-64	65+

Purpose can appear in the subtlest forms. For some people, it's spending time with their children. Others find it tending a garden, or volunteering at a local food bank or homeless shelter. Everyone's purpose is different, so there's no right answer to the question of where to find it. Purpose is simply whatever brings you the greatest meaning or joy.

When you find it, things shift. You're in the flow. Tasks feel effortless. Big things begin to happen.

Chapter 7

Igniting a Middlescent Revolution

Middlescence, a newly identified life stage, born of the realities of living in the 21st century, is ripe with power and potential. Even though we live in an imperfect world, we can harness our creativity, leadership and focus to forge a vibrant, exciting mid-life. When we do so, it's a gift to our family, our community, our workplace and the world. But most of all, it has the power to revolutionize our lives.

My promise to you

Visit my site for more tools and information to shape your mid-dlesence:

http://www.barbarawaxman.com/TheMiddlescenceFactor

I am creating a movement to transform midlife into a Mid-dlescent Revolution. Become a part of the middlescence community by joining us on Facebook:

https://www.facebook.com/TheMiddlescenceFactor/

Barbara Waxman

About Barbara Waxman

Barbara Waxman is a gerontologist, leadership coach, and speaker whose insights are illuminating a crucial stage in our personal and professional lives: Middlescence. Between ages 45 and 65, right when we should be embracing life at the peak and taking advantage of our hard-earned wisdom, we often find ourselves tangled in questions about where we've been and what's next. In her forthcoming book, she shows how this new life stage can be a powerful period of self-actualization and an invaluable opportunity to reset our goals, our strategies, and our sense of what really matters. In adolescence, we all experienced a major transition in who we were and how we saw the world. In Middlescence, we encounter another major change, but this time we can marshal the wisdom and wherewithal to take full advantage of the promise of this life stage. As one of the foremost gerontologist coaches in the United States, Barbara is known for inspiring clients and listeners with insights so that they can be effective in planning for themselves and their leadership at home, at work, and in their communities.

BARBARA WAXMAN BIOGRAPHY

Certified by both the International Coach Federation and The Hudson Institute, Barbara holds Masters Degrees in Both Administration and Gerontology and is a Wexner Heritage Foundation Fellow. Barbara blogs for Huff/Post 50, NextAvenue, Forbes.com, Sixty and Me, and VibrantNation. Her work has been featured in SmartMoney.com, Fortune, Newsday, U.S. News & World Report, AARP The Magazine, and more. In consulting and coaching, she brings personal and professional experience to an effective, results-oriented collaboration. Her ability to inspire others with compassion, honesty and a light heart, while incorporating cutting edge leadership principles, distinguishes Barbara's work.

Originally from New York, Barbara lives in Northern California, though in 2015 she and her husband, Scott, spent the year "repotting" in Italy. Barbara's community involvement includes work with various non-profits including SHE-CAN and Beyond Differences. She is a lifelong learner who loves hiking, cooking, yoga and stepping just outside of her comfort zone.

barbara@barbarawaxman.com
www.barbarawaxman.com

Solutions from The Middlescence Factor©

The Middlescent Leader

A proprietary one-on-one coaching model developed over years of working with high performing people. Entrepreneurship Turned Inward (ETI)© is focused on your leadership roles, and leverages research from the fields of high performance, adult development, positive psychology and more.

Life Coaching

One-on-one coaching for the 24/7 version of you. This engaging and active process helps you feel like you are thriving, happier and more effective.

Workshops

Create a working session, based on the needs of your YPO, Vistage Group, company or organization, designed to engage participants with tools, skill-building, and an action plan for designing a life where you can Thrive!

Speaking

Engage Barbara to speak to your organization. Contact her at barbara@barbarawaxman.com to discuss your audience and potential topics.

To learn more about The Middlescence Factor:

Call: (415) 461–3610

Write: barbara@barbarawaxman.com

Visit: www.barbarawaxman.com

Made in the USA
Lexington, KY
30 April 2019